27th February 2017

To Sophie,

Thank you for giving me the opportunity to serve in such an important role of a "Mother, to Hugo". Please accept this book, my book as a token of gratitude for trusting us and for all your support. Enjoy!

With love + Best wishes
from

Yasmin

Yasmin's Kitchen

Wonderful tastes from my kitchen

Recipes, Foreword & Contents
by
Yasmin Hunt-Bhamla

Design & Editing
by
Yasmin Hunt-Bhamla, Farook Bhamla & Adnaan Bhamla

First Edition
All Rights Reserved ©2015 Yasmin Hunt-Bhamla

www.yasminhuntbhamla.com

Contents

Foreword — Page 7

A to Z of Herbs and Spices — Page 8-13

Useful Information — Page 14-15

Soups and Starters — Page 16

Meat and Poultry — Page 24

Fish and Shellfish — Page 38

Rice — Page 46

Cakes, Desserts and Perfect Pastry — Page 50

Index — Page 58-59

Foreword

Everything I know about cooking I have learnt through hard work, passion and watching other people cook.

Cooking at home throws up a different set of challenges to that of a professional chef in a Michelin starred restaurant.

If you are expecting Michelin quality food from this cookbook, you will be sorely disappointed. My food is more rustic and easy going. But family and friends can be the most demanding people to cook for and never afraid to tell you what they think.

So what do we want from home cooking ?

I think the answer is the same in every home.

With a busy household, there's me, Farook and our son, Adnaan . I want things to be relaxed. I want to use fresh ingredients. I want to provide healthy food, as quickly and efficiently as possible. I want it to be the kind of food that gets people excited. I want the sort of food that will draw the whole family together, sitting around a table sharing food and conversation is one of the greatest pleasures in life.

Most of the dishes included in this book have been picked up on my travels to various parts of the world and "made them my own". Some have been passed down to me by family and friends. Therefore this book is a representation of my culinary knowledge over the years. This knowledge has increased my expertise in cooking to the extent that I feel I am a worthy disciple.

Cooking is not a mystery art. The secret of good cooking is a love of good food.

My thanks to my family for their sustained help, encouragement, warmth and love. Without them a book of this nature could not be possible.

Good Luck, good cooking, and most of all good eating.

Yasmin

A to Z of Herbs and Spices

Dried Herbs and Spices

Asafoetida (Asafetida) - Used as a digestive aid in Indian cooking and has a strong odour that mellows out into a garlic-onion flavour.

Achiote Paste and Powder - Reddish-brown paste or powder ground from annatto seeds with an earthy flavour. Used primarily in Mexican dishes like mole sauce, cochinita pibil and tamales.

Allspice - Similar to cloves but more pungent and deeply flavoured. Best used in spice mixes.

Annatto Seeds - A very tough reddish-brown seed with a woodsy aroma and an earthy flavour. Called Achiote Paste (see above) when ground, this is used to flavour many Mexican dishes.

Bay Leaf - *(also: Indian Bay Leaf)* Adds a woodsy background note to soups and sauces.

Biber Flakes - used in Turkish cooking. A rich, fruity crushed pepper.

Caraway Seed - These anise-tasting seeds are essential for soda bread, sauerkraut and potato salad.

Cardamon - This warm, aromatic spice is widely used in Indian cuisine. It's also great in baked goods when used in combination with spices like clove and cinnamon.

Cayenne Pepper - Made from dried and ground red chilli peppers. Adds a sweet heat to soups, braises, and spice mixes.

Chia Seeds - Nearly flavourless, they can be ground into smoothies, cereals and baked goods for extra nutrition and texture or even used as a vegan egg substitute.

Cinnamon - *(also: Vietnamese Cassia Cinnamon)* Used in worldwide cuisine and doubles up as a spice in both sweet and savoury dishes.

Cloves - Sweet and warming spice. Used most often in baking, but also good with braised meat.

Coriander Seed - Earthy, lemony flavour. Used in a lot of Mexican and Indian dishes.

Cumin - Smoky and earthy. Used in a lot of Southwestern US, Mexican, North African, Middle Eastern and Indian cuisine.

Fennel Seed - Lightly sweet and licorice flavoured. It is excellent with meat dishes or chewed on its own as a breath freshener and digestion aid.

Fenugreek - Although this herb smells like maple syrup while cooking, it has a rather bitter, burnt sugar flavour. Found in a lot of Indian and Middle Eastern dishes.

Garlic Powder - Garlic powder is made from dehydrated garlic cloves and can be used to give dishes a sweeter, softer garlic flavour.

Ginger - Ground ginger is made from dehydrated fresh ginger and has a spicy, zesty bite.

Gochugaru - This Korean red pepper spice is hot, sweet and slightly smoky.

Grains of Paradise - These taste like a cross between cardamon, citrus and black pepper. They add a warming note to many North African dishes.

Kaffir Lime Leaves - Used to flavour curries and many Thai dishes. Can be sold fresh, dry or frozen.

Loomi - Also called black lime, this is ground from dried limes. Adds a sour kick to many Middle Eastern dishes.

Mace - From the same plant as nutmeg, but tastes more subtle and delicate. Great in savoury dishes, especially stews and homemade sausages.

Mahlab - Ground from sour cherry pits, this spice has a nutty and somewhat sour flavour. It is used in a lot of sweet breads throughout the Middle East.

Nutmeg - Sweet and pungent. Great in baked goods, but also adds a warm note to savoury dishes.

Nutritional Yeast - Very different from bread yeast, this can be sprinkled onto or into sauces, pastas and other dishes to add a nutty, cheesy, savoury flavour.

Paprika - Adds a sweet note and a red colour. Used in stews and spice blends. There is also a spicy version labelled hot paprika.

Oregano - Robust, somewhat lemony flavour. Used in a lot of Mexican and Mediterranean dishes.

Peppercorns - Peppercorns come in a variety of colours: black, white, pink and green being the most popular. These are pungent and pack a mild heat.

Rosemary - Strong and piney. Great with eggs, beans, and potatoes, as well as grilled meats.

Saffron - Saffron has a subtle but distinct floral flavour and aroma. It also gives food a bright yellow colour.

Sage - Pine-like flavour, with more lemony and eucalyptus notes than rosemary. Found in a lot of northern Italian cooking.

Dried Herbs and Spices continued

Smoked Paprika – Adds sweet smokiness to dishes and a red colour.

Star Anise - Whole star anise can be used to add a sweet licorice flavour to sauces and soups.

Sumac - Zingy and lemony. It is a Middle Eastern spice. Great in marinades, spice rubs and as a salad dressing.

Turmeric - Sometimes used more for its yellow colour than its flavour. It has a mild woody flavour. Can be used instead of saffron for those on a budget.

Thyme - Adds a pungent, woody flavour. Great for all purpose seasoning.

Vietnamese Cassia Cinnamon - *(also: Cinnamon)* Sweet and spicy. Can be used in both sweet baked goods and to add depth to savoury dishes.

Fresh Herbs

Basil - *(also: Thai Basil)* Highly aromatic with a robust licorice flavour. Excellent in pestos, as a finishing touch on pasta dishes or stuffed into sandwiches.

Chervil - Delicate anise flavour. Great raw in salads or as a finishing garnish.

Chives - Delicate onion flavour, great as a garnish or in sour cream dips.

Cilantro - From the coriander plant, cilantro leaves and stems have a pungent, herbaceous flavour. Used in Caribbean, Latin American and Asian cooking.

Curry Leaves - These pungent leaves are not related to curry powder but release a similar flavour. Used in Indian, Malaysian, Sri Lankan, Singaporean, and Pakistani cuisine. Used to flavour curries, soups, stews and chutneys.

Dill - Light and feathery herb with a pungent herb flavour. Use it for pickling, with fish and over potatoes.

Fenugreek - Although this herb smells like maple syrup while cooking, it has a rather bitter, burnt sugar flavour. Found in a lot of Indian and Middle Eastern dishes.

Lemon Thyme - *(also: Thyme)* Sweet lemon aroma and a fresh lemony-herbal flavour. This is excellent with poultry and in vinaigrettes.

Lovage - Tastes like a cross between celery and parsley. Great with seafood or to flavour stocks and soups.

Marjoram - Floral and woody. Try it in sauces, vinaigrettes and marinades.

Mint - Surprisingly versatile for such an intensely flavoured herb. Try it with lamb, peas, potatoes - and with chocolate.

Oregano - Robust, somewhat lemony flavour. Used in a lot of Mexican and Mediterranean dishes.

Parsley - Available in flat-leaf (Italian) or curly varieties. This very popular herb is light and grassy in flavour.

Pink Pepper - Small and sweet, these are fantastic when marinated with olives or simply sprinkled on shortbread.

Rosemary - Strong and piney. Great with eggs, beans, potatoes and grilled meats.

Sage - Pine-like flavour, with more lemony and eucalyptus notes than rosemary. Found in a lot of northern Italian cooking.

Summer Savoury - Peppery green flavour similar to thyme. Mostly used in roasted meat dishes and stuffing, but also goes well with beans.

Shiso - A member of the mint family, this herb is used extensively in Japanese, Korean, and South East Asian cooking as a wrap for steaming fish and vegetables, in soups, and as a general seasoning.

Tarragon - Strong anise flavour. Can be eaten raw in salads or used to flavour tomato dishes, chicken, seafood or eggs.

Thai Basil - *(also: Basil)* A spicy, edgier cousin to sweet Italian basil. A must have for Thai stir fries, Vietnamese pho, spring rolls and other South Asian dishes.

Thyme - *(also: Lemon Thyme)* Adds a pungent, woody flavour. Great as an all-purpose seasoning.

Spice Blends, Rubs & Mixes

Baharat - Black pepper, cumin, cinnamon and cloves. Used to flavour soups, tomato sauces, lentils, rice pilafs, couscous and can be a rub for meats. (Middle Eastern)

Bebere - Hot peppers, black pepper, fenugreek, ginger, cardamon, coriander, cinnamon and cloves. Other ingredients may include ajwain, cumin, allspice, nutmeg, paprika, onion or garlic. Used to flavour slow cooked stews. (African)

Bouquet Garni - Thyme, parsley and bay leaf. Used to flavour broths and soups. (Classic French)

Chilli Powder - Ground chillies, cumin, oregano, cayenne and lots of optional extras to make this seasoning uniquely yours. Use for chilli stew, beans, grilled meat and tacos. (Mexican/ Southwestern US)

Chinese Five-Spice Powder - Star anise, Szechuan peppercorns, fennel, cassia and clove. Adds sweetness and depth to savoury dishes, especially beef, duck and pork. (Chinese)

Curry Powder - Typically includes turmeric, coriander, cumin, fenugreek and red pepper, but mixes can vary. Used primarily to quickly flavour curry sauces. (Indian)

Dukkah - Includes nuts (most often hazelnuts), sesame seeds, coriander and cumin. Great spice rub for lamb, chicken and fish. (Egyptian)

Garam Masala - Typically includes cinnamon, cardamon, cloves, cumin, coriander, nutmeg and pepper. Sweeter than curry powder. Also used to season curry sauces. (Indian)

Herbes De Provence - Usually savoury, rosemary, marjoram, thyme and sometimes lavender. Use as a marinade or dry rub for roast chicken, fish and vegetables. (French)

Old Bay - Celery salt, mustard, red and black pepper, bay leaves, cloves, allspice, ginger, mace, cardamon, cinnamon and paprika. Created in the Chesapeake Bay area of Maryland, it is traditionally used for shrimp and crab.

Pickling Spice - Most often, bay leaf, yellow mustard seeds, black peppercorns, allspice and coriander. Used for pickling vegetables in vinegar.

Pumpkin Pie Spice Mix - Cinnamon, nutmeg, ginger and cloves. Used for seasoning pumpkin pie, but also great in other spiced baked goods.

Ras el Hanout - Cardamon, clove, cinnamon, paprika, coriander, cumin, mace, nutmeg, peppercorn and turmeric. Use as a spice rub on meat or a simple condiment. (North African/Moroccan)

Shichimi Togarashi - Although the ingredients vary, they typically include sansho or Sichuan pepper, dried citrus peel, sesame seeds, poppy seeds, hemp seeds, ginger, garlic, shiso and nori. Used on noodles and grilled meats. (Japanese)

Za'atar Seasoning Blend - Thyme, sumac and sesame seeds. All-purpose seasoning for many Middle Eastern dishes like grilled meats, grilled vegetables, flatbread and hummus. (Middle Eastern)

Quick Cookery Tip

When using Ginger/Garlic paste, use the quantity mix of 2 parts ginger to 1 part garlic.
Peel and roughly chop both, whiz in a food processor and freeze until needed.
Minced fresh chillies can be frozen in the same way !
Saves so much time!

USEFUL INFORMATION

Metric cup & spoon sizes

cup	metric
¼ cup	60ml
⅓ cup	80ml
½ cup	125ml
1 cup	250ml

spoon	metric
¼ tsp	1.25ml
½ tsp	2.50ml
1 tsp	5ml
2 tsp	10ml
1 tbsp (4 tsp)	20ml

Oven temperatures

Electric	Fahrenheit	Gas
120°	250°	1
150°	300°	2
160°	325°	3
180°	350°	4
190°	375°	5
200°	400°	6
230°	450°	7
250°	500°	9

Soups and Starters

Prawn and Sweetcorn Chowder

Serves 6-8

Ingredients

400g prawns
1 small green pepper, sliced and diced
1 onion, finely chopped
350g potatoes peeled and diced
250g sweetcorn
25g butter
1 tbsp plain flour
450ml single cream
450ml fish stock
Salt & ground black pepper
Pinch of ground nutmeg
Pinch cayenne pepper

Directions

1. Seed and chop the pepper into small pieces.

2. Peel the potatoes and dice in the same way.

3. Heat the butter in a large pan and when melted add the onions, potatoes and pepper and fry gently for about 7 or 8 minutes until softened. Stirring occasionally.

4. Sprinkle the flour over the frying vegetables, stirring for a few minutes until the mixture is golden and frothy.

5. Add the seasoning and spices to the pan.

6. Blend the fish stock with the cream and add this to the pan, bring to the boil, cover and reduce heat to a simmer for 15 minutes until the vegetables are tender.

7. Stir the prawns into the pan along with the sweetcorn.

8. Cook for a few minutes until the prawns are cooked or heated through. But not tough and rubbery.

9. Adjust the seasoning to suit and serve with crusty bread.

Leek and Chickpea Soup

Serves 4-6

Ingredients

2 large tins of chickpeas
1 medium potato peeled and chopped
5 medium leeks
1 tablespoon olive oil
knob of butter
1 tsp ginger/garlic paste
salt and freshly ground black pepper
850ml chicken or vegetable stock
Parmesan cheese

Directions

1. Cover the potatoes with water and cook until tender. Remove the outer skin of the leeks and slice lengthways from the root up. Then wash carefully and slice finely.

2. Warm a thick bottomed pan and add the tablespoon of oil and the knob of butter. Add the leeks and garlic to the pan and sweat gently with a good pinch of salt until tender and sweet.

3. Add the drained chickpeas and potato and cook for 1 minute. Add about two-thirds of the stock and simmer for 15 minutes.

4. Puree half and leave the other half whole - this gives a lovely smooth comforting feel but also keeps a bit of texture.

5. Now add enough of the remaining stock to achieve the consistency you like.

Season to taste, and add Parmesan.

(Red Lentil Soup)

Serves 6

Ingredients

1 ½ cups of red lentils
8 cups of meat stock
1 cup water
2 medium onions chopped
1 tbsp margarine/coconut oil
Season to taste . I use a mixture of salt, ground black pepper and biber flakes

Directions

1. Wash the lentils.

2. Melt the margarine in a saucepan. Add the onions and fry lightly until soft.

3. Add the lentils and the stock and cook until soft. Approximately 35 minutes in a saucepan or 10 minutes in a pressure cooker.

4. Blend until smooth.

5. Season to taste.

6. Serve with crusty bread, topped with melted cheese.

Hummus

Serves 6

Ingredients

400g tin chickpeas drained
2 tbsp lemon juice
1 tbsp olive oil
2-3 tbsp water
1 tsp parsley
1 clove garlic

Directions

1. Puree all the ingredients together in a food processor or blender until smooth.

2. Season to taste with salt and pepper.

3. Serve with crudités or crusty bread.

Chilli Pumpkin or Butternut Squash Soup

Serves 6

Ingredients

50g butter
1 large chopped onion
4 spring onions chopped
2 tomatoes peeled and chopped
2 cloves of garlic crushed
2 fresh chillies chopped
225g sweet potato peeled and cubed
1.1kg/2lb 8oz pumpkin/Squash peeled, seeded and cubed
1.7 litres/3 pints beef stock
1 tsp sugar
salt and ground pepper
fresh cream
grated parmesan

Directions

1. Melt the butter in a large pan. Add the garlic, chillies, spring onions and onions. Cook until softened.

2. Stir in the tomatoes, sweet potatoes and pumpkin and cook for 5 minutes.

3. Pour in the stock and the sugar then season to taste.

4. Bring to boil, reduce the heat and simmer with the lid on for 25 to 30 minutes, until the pumpkin is soft.

5. Remove from the heat. Allow to cool slightly before liquidising.

6. Heat for a few minutes and adjust seasoning. Swirl in some cream and add the parmesan if desired.

7. Serve with crusty bread.

Meat & Poultry

Spicy Chicken Breast in Semolina

Serves 4

Ingredients

*500g chicken breast, thinly sliced steaks
*1 heaped tsp ginger/garlic paste
* ½ tsp minced chilli
*1 tsp ground coriander
*1 tsp ground cumin
*1 tsp salt
*1 tbsp lemon juice
* ¼ tsp dried coriander
fine semolina
2/3 beaten eggs

Directions

1. Mix all the ingredients marked with *. Cover the sliced chicken breasts and marinate for at least 1 hour.

2. Cover the marinated breasts in semolina.

3. Coat in the beaten egg.

4. Shallow fry in a little oil till golden brown, turning regularly.

Spicy Kidneys

Serves 4

Ingredients

500g kidneys (washed, skinned & cored)
2 tbsp oil
¼ fresh minced green chilli
1 tsp salt
1 tsp ginger/garlic paste
1 tsp coriander
⅛ tsp turmeric

Directions

1. Mix all the spices with the kidneys.

2. Fry in the oil.

3. Cook on low heat for 1-1 ½ hours, stirring regularly. Add water to stop it from sticking.

4. Serve on crusty bread.

Spicy Lamb Chops

Serves 4-6

Ingredients

500g lamb chops

1 tbsp olive oil

1 tbsp lemon juice

1 tbsp ginger/garlic paste

¼ tsp minced chilli

1 tbsp Schwartz perfect shake steak herb and spice blend

1 tsp salt

water to cover the chops

Directions

1. Marinate the chops in the oil, lemon juice, ginger/garlic paste, chilli, steak seasoning and salt for at least 2 hours.

2. Place the marinated chops in a roasting tin and add enough water to nearly cover the chops.

3. Preheat the oven on the highest setting.

4. Cover the roasting tin completely with foil making sure there are no gaps. This ensures that some moisture stays in the tin and the chops do not dry out. Place in the oven between the bottom and middle shelf and cook on the highest setting for 1½ hours.

6. After 1½ hours remove the foil and continue to cook uncovered for 30 minutes, stirring the "sauce" and turning the chops every 10 minutes. The chops will be very tender and you will have a lovely thick sauce to either add to your gravy or for dipping your roast potatoes or chops in.

Masala Aloo

Serves 4-6

Ingredients

4 large potatoes
1 tsp ginger/garlic paste
3 onions
1 tsp salt
¼ heaped tsp minced chilli
⅛ tsp turmeric
½ heaped tsp mustard seeds
1 tbsp coconut oil
1 tbsp chopped coriander leaf
2 tbsp desiccated coconut

Directions

1. Boil or steam the potatoes till just done. Once cooled chop the potatoes into cubes.

2. Heat 1 tbsp of coconut oil in a pan or wok. Add the mustard seeds. When they have stopped spluttering add the sliced onions and fry until golden brown.

3. Add all the spices and seasonings then fry for a few moments.

4. Add the cubed potatoes and blend well, trying not to mash up the potatoes.

Popcorn Chicken Strips

Serves 4

Ingredients

4 Chicken breasts cut in strips
50g salted popcorn
160g stale breadcrumbs
1 ½ tsp paprika
75g plain flour
2 large eggs
Oil for frying
Salt and pepper

Zingy Sour Cream Dip
200ml soured cream
Zest of 1 lime and its juice
Chopped coriander

Sour Cream and Chive Dip
Small carton of sour cream
good pinch chopped chives
Salt & pepper-season to taste
Pinch of cayenne pepper

Directions

1. Place the popcorn, breadcrumbs and paprika in a food processor. Blend until finely chopped. Tip into a wide shallow bowl. Whisk the eggs in a second bowl. Mix the flour with some seasoning in a third bowl.

2. Dip the chicken strips first into the seasoned flour, then into the egg mixture, and finally into the popcorn breadcrumbs – press the crumbs onto the chicken to help them stick. Continue until all the chicken pieces are coated, and then chill for 30 mins, or up to 1 day.

3. Mix together the ingredients for the dip in a small bowl.

4. When you're ready to cook the chicken, heat enough oil to just cover the surface of a large frying pan. Once hot cook the chicken pieces for approximately 5 mins on each side (in batches so you don't overcrowd the pan) until golden and cooked through.

5. Drain on kitchen paper. Serve with zingy sour cream dip, sour cream and chive dip or sweet chilli dip on the side.

Kofte Kebabs

Makes 24

Ingredients

500g lamb mince
1 onion grated
1 tbsp chopped coriander leaves
1 tsp mint
1 tbsp ginger/garlic paste
1 tsp salt
¼ tsp cayenne pepper
¼ tsp ground cinnamon

Directions

1. Place all the ingredients, except the oil, in a large bowl and mix well using your hands.

2. Divide the mixture into 24 equal balls and place on a flat tray and chill for at least 1 hour or freeze until needed.

3. Put a little oil into a large pan and lightly fry. Turning frequently until done. About 7-10 mins each side.

4. Serve with rice, salad and sour cream dip.

Serves 4-6

Ingredients

500g minced meat
2 small grated onions
3 slices crustless bread
400g tin chopped tomatoes
1 pinch of biber flakes
1 heaped tsp of ginger/garlic paste
1 tsp salt
½ tsp ground black pepper
¾ tsp ground cumin
2 chopped peppers
2 tbsp oil
1 extra onion chopped finely
extra seasoning
300ml meat stock
extra 1 tsp of ginger/garlic paste for sauce

Directions

1. Soak the bread slices in water.

2. Squeeze the bread by hand to extract the excess water.

3. Crumble the bread and add to the minced meat together with the grated onions, ginger/garlic, salt, pepper and cumin.

4. Mix well and shape into walnut size pieces. Rolling each in the palms of your hands into a round and slightly flatten.

5. Freeze or refrigerate for about 1-2 hours to firm up.

6. Heat the oil in a pan and fry the chopped onions and peppers with 1 tsp ginger/garlic paste until soft and lightly browned.

7. Add the tin tomatoes, 300ml meat stock, pinch of biber flakes and season to taste.

8. Place the firm "Kofte" into the sauce and cook for approximately 20 to 30 minutes on a low heat, stirring occasionally, being careful not to break up the Kofte. Cubed potatoes or potato wedges can be added if you wish.

9. Serve with rice, spaghetti or crusty bread.

Grilled Spiced Moroccan Chicken

Serves 4-6

Ingredients

500g Chicken (small chicken drumsticks or thighs, chopped chicken breast, wings or niblets)
*1- 2 heaped Tsp ginger/garlic paste
*1 tsp salt
*1 tsp paprika
*1 tsp ground cumin
*½ tsp ground coriander
*½ tsp ground black pepper
*¼ tsp cayenne pepper
*1 tbsp lemon juice
*1 tbsp olive oil
*1 tbsp fresh/dried coriander leaves
*1 pinch/drop of red food colouring
chopped coriander leaf and 1 lemon cut into wedges for serving

Directions

1. In a bowl, mix all the ingredients marked with a * into a well mixed paste.

2. Smear the chicken portions with the paste.

3. Cover with cling film and marinate for at least 2 hours.

4. Add the marinated chicken to a wok, fry pan or sauté pan.

5. Add just the right amount of water to stop it sticking and cook until chicken is done, ensuring that there is enough liquid/sauce in the pan to stop it from burning. Adding more water if needed.

6. You should have a nice thick coating sauce.

7. Once done serve with lemon wedges.

Chicken Madras

Serves 4-6

Ingredients

4 chicken breasts
3 tbsp vegetable or coconut oil
2 onions peeled and finely chopped
1 tsp ginger/garlic paste
1 tsp sea salt and black pepper
400g tin chopped tomatoes
300ml water
½ tsp garam masala
coriander leaves to garnish
½ tsp of minced green chilli
2 tsp ground cumin
1 tsp ground coriander
¼ tsp ground turmeric
½ –2 tsp (or more!) hot chilli powder, to taste
6–8 curry leaves

Directions

1. Cut the chicken into strips or cubes and put aside. Heat the oil and add the onions and cook until they start to soften which will be about 5 or 6 mins.

2. Once the onions have started to brown add the chillies, the garlic and ginger and cook for a further 2-3 minutes. Then add the salt, pepper, turmeric, cumin, coriander, curry leaves and chilli powder and leave to cook for a further minute or so.

3. Add the chicken to the pan and cook until the chicken begins to go golden brown all over, stirring regularly.

4. Add the water and the chopped tomatoes and then bring to boil. Once the pan is boiling, reduce the heat to a simmer and cover the pan stirring every so often.

5. Let it simmer for about 30 minutes and add more water as needed if it begins to stick or the sauce becomes too dry. Remember to stir well if you do need to add water.

6. At the end of the 30 minutes stir in the garam masala and leave uncovered for another 10 minutes, again taking care not to let it dry out.

7. Serve with basmati rice.

Moroccan Leg of Lamb

Serves 4-6

Ingredients

1 leg of lamb (about 2 kg)
*1 heaped tsp ginger/garlic paste
*1 tsp salt
*4 tsp ground coriander
*2 tsp ground cumin
*1 tsp paprika
*¼ tsp cayenne pepper
*3 tbsp ghee or soft butter

1 ½ tbsp ground cumin mixed with 2 tsp salt for serving

Directions

1. In a small bowl mix all the ingredients marked with a * until it is a well mixed paste.

2. Place the lamb leg on a baking tray or pan.

3. Smear the paste onto the lamb leg using a palette knife to spread all over the lamb.

4. Cover with cling film and marinate for at least 2 hours or overnight in a refrigerator.

5. Pre heat the oven to Gas Mark 4 (360F, 180C).

6. Remove the cling film and cover with foil, trying not to touch the marinated lamb.

7. Bake the leg on a centre shelf for 1 ½ hours.

8. Remove the foil and baste the lamb with the fat in the pan.

9. Leave uncovered and reduce the heat to Gas mark 3 (325F, 170C).

10. Bake for a further 2 to 3 hours, basting every 30 minutes, to keep the lamb moist.

11. The low heat and long cooking browns the lamb without burning the spices and cooks it to melting tenderness. Lamb must be well done. Once done, carve at the table. Serve with roast potatoes, vegetables and/or a salad and small individual bowls of the cumin/salt mixture.

Thai Green Chicken or Prawn Curry

Ingredients

A large handful of baby corn
½ a fresh red chilli
1 tbsp groundnut oil
1 tbsp sesame oil
400g chicken breast (or 400g prawns)
1 x 400ml tin of coconut milk
Handful of mange tout
1 lime

Serves 4

<u>For the green curry paste:</u>
2 stalks of lemongrass
4 spring onions
3 fresh green chillies
1 tsp ginger/garlic paste
A large bunch of fresh coriander
1 tsp coriander seeds
8 dried lime leaves
2 tbsp soy sauce
1 tbsp fish sauce

Directions

To make your green curry paste:

1. Trim the lemongrass stalks, peel back and discard the outer leaves, and crush the stalks by bashing them a few times with the heel of your hand or a rolling pin.

2. Trim the spring onions. Halve and de-seed the green chillies.

3. Set aside a few sprigs of fresh coriander and whiz the rest in a food processor with the lemongrass stalks, spring onions, chillies, garlic, ginger, coriander seeds and lime leaves until everything is finely chopped .
While whizzing pour in the soy sauce and fish sauce and blitz again until you have a smooth paste. If you don't have a food processor, chop everything by hand as finely as you can.

To make your curry:

4. Finely chop the red chilli and put to one side.

5. Place a large pan or wok over a high heat. When it is really hot, add the groundnut and sesame oils, stirring continuously, then add the chicken or prawns. Add the baby corn and your green curry paste and stir fry for about 30 seconds.

6. Pour in the coconut milk and add the mange tout. Give it all a good stir, bring to the boil and cook until the chicken or prawns are thoroughly cooked. Have a taste and add a bit more soy sauce if you think it needs it.

7. Push down on the lime and roll it around to get the juices going, and then cut the lime in half. Squeeze the juice into the pan.

8. Serve with basmati rice.

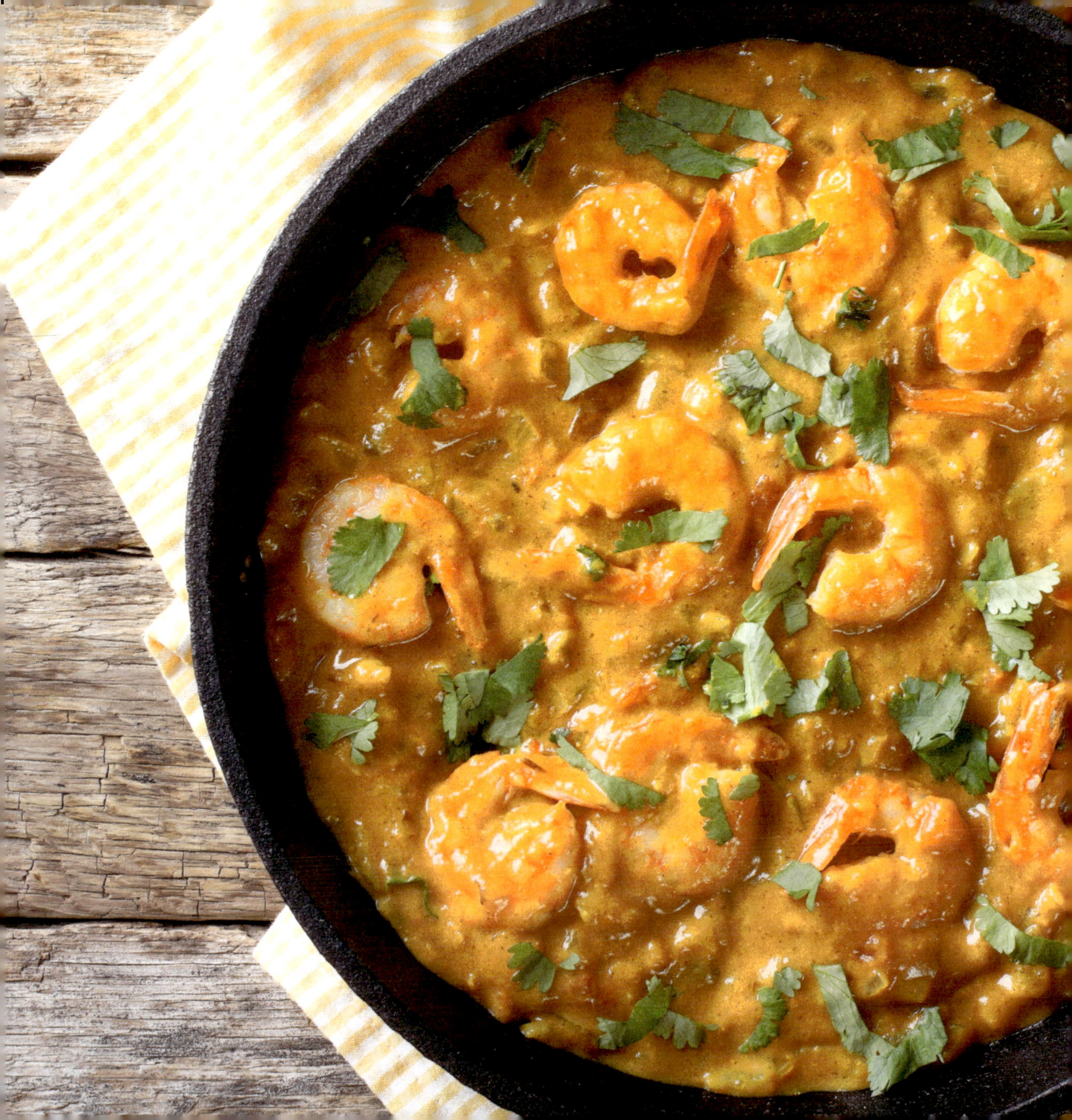

Fish & Shellfish

Marinated Tuna Steaks

Serves 4

Ingredients

4 Tuna Steaks
Coconut Oil

For the marinade:
4 tbsp light soy sauce
1 tbsp of lemon juice
¼ tsp chopped/minced green chilli
1 tsp of minced ginger/garlic

Directions

1. Combine all the marinade ingredients in a shallow bowl large enough to take the steaks.

2. Marinate the steaks for at least 1 hour.

3. Pre-heat a griddle or non-stick frying pan and add a light coating of coconut oil.

4. When the pan is hot add the steaks and cook for 2 to 3 minutes each side. Do not overcook the steaks or the texture will be tough and dry. Serve hot.

Bengali Prawn Curry

Serves 4

Ingredients

400g prawns
⅛ tsp ground turmeric
Salt
2 chopped onions
1 tsp ginger/garlic paste
¼ - ½ tsp minced green chilli
2 tbsp coconut oil
1 tsp mustard seeds
2 whole cloves
2 green cardamom pods
1 small piece of cinnamon stick
2 bay leaves
400ml tin coconut milk
2 tbsp water

Directions

1. Put the onions, ginger/garlic, chillies, turmeric, salt and the water into a blender/food processor and blend into a fine, wet paste.

2. Heat the coconut oil in a large pan or wok.

3. Add the mustard seeds, cloves, cinnamon stick, cardamom and bay leaves.

4. Fry until the mustard seeds start to sputter and the spices are fragrant.

5. Add the wet paste and fry over a low heat for 12-15 minutes, stirring often to avoid sticking.

6. Add the coconut milk.

7. Add the prawns and gently simmer over a low heat for 2-3 minutes until they are cooked through.

8. Serve with plain white rice.

Serves 4

Ingredients

4 fish fillets about 400g-500g (I use Basa fillets but any firm fish will do)
3 tbsp of toasted sesame oil
1 tsp ginger/garlic paste
¼ to ½ tsp minced green chilli
⅛ tsp turmeric
1 x 400g tin of chopped tomatoes
Pinch of caster sugar
Small bunch of coriander leaves (plus extra to garnish)
1 tsp salt and ground black pepper to taste
1 large potato (about 300g) peeled and diced
200ml water

Directions

1. Heat the oil in a wok or non-stick frying pan.

2. Add the fish fillets and fry until just cooked through (about 2-3 minutes each side).

3. Remove from the pan and set aside until later.

4. Add the spices and seasoning to the pan. Fry for a few minutes.

5. Then add the water, turn the heat down to a simmer and add the tomatoes and diced potato and season to taste.

6. Cook on low heat for about 15 minutes until the potatoes are tender.

7. Return the cooked fillets to the pan and gently heat until warmed through.

8. Garnish with some chopped coriander leaves and serve with basmati rice.

Yasmin's Thai Fish Cakes

Makes 12

Ingredients

400g of white fish fillets (I prefer to use Basa, but any firm white fish will do)
250g mashed potatoes (I use the ready made frozen variety)
½ tsp minced green chilli
1 tsp ginger/garlic paste
1 tsp ground cumin
1 tsp ground coriander
Small handful of coriander leaves, finely chopped or 1tsp of dried coriander leaves
⅛ tsp turmeric
1 tsp salt
Ground black pepper to taste
Small amount of milk (to poach the fish)

Directions

1. Add the fish to the pan.

2. Add the milk to the pan so that it nearly covers the fish to stop it from sticking.

3. Poach until just cooked through.

4. Remove the fillets from the milk and leave to cool. Discard the milk.

5. In a bowl add the mashed potato, spices and seasoning.

6. Add the fish and lightly flake into the potato mixture.

7. Mix well.

8. With damp hands (I use vinyl gloves) divide into 12 patties and shape into round, flat "cakes".

9. Place on a baking tray covered in cling film and place in the freezer for at least 1 hour. The fish cakes can be cooked from frozen if preferred.

10. Grill the fish cakes, turning regularly, until golden brown and thoroughly cooked through.

11. Serve with Turkish rice and sweet chilli sauce.

Yasmin's Ginger Beer Battered Fish

Ingredients

4 chunky fish fillets (Cod, Haddock, etc) skinless and boneless
A pinch of salt and ground black pepper

Serves 4

For the batter:
225g plain flour
2 tsp baking powder
1 tbsp of flavourless oil
A pinch of cayenne pepper
300ml ginger beer
An additional handful of flour and a pinch of salt & black pepper

Directions

1. Season the fish with a little salt and black pepper. Cover and chill for 10 minutes.

2. Sift the flour in a bowl and add the baking powder, cayenne pepper, oil, ginger beer an additional pinch of salt and a little black pepper, stirring as you add each ingredient.

3. Continue to stir the mixture until it resembles double cream.

4. Leave to stand for 30 minutes.

5. Heat the oil over a medium heat, allowing the oil to heat up to 160 C.

6. Put the additional handful of flour and salt/pepper on a plate and coat each fillet in the seasoned flour, shaking off any excess.

7. Give the batter a stir. Dip and coat each fillet, ensuring any excess is allowed to drip off.

8. Fry for approximately 5 minutes, depending on the thickness of the fillets, until the batter is golden, dark and crisp. Lift out with a slotted spoon and drain on kitchen paper.

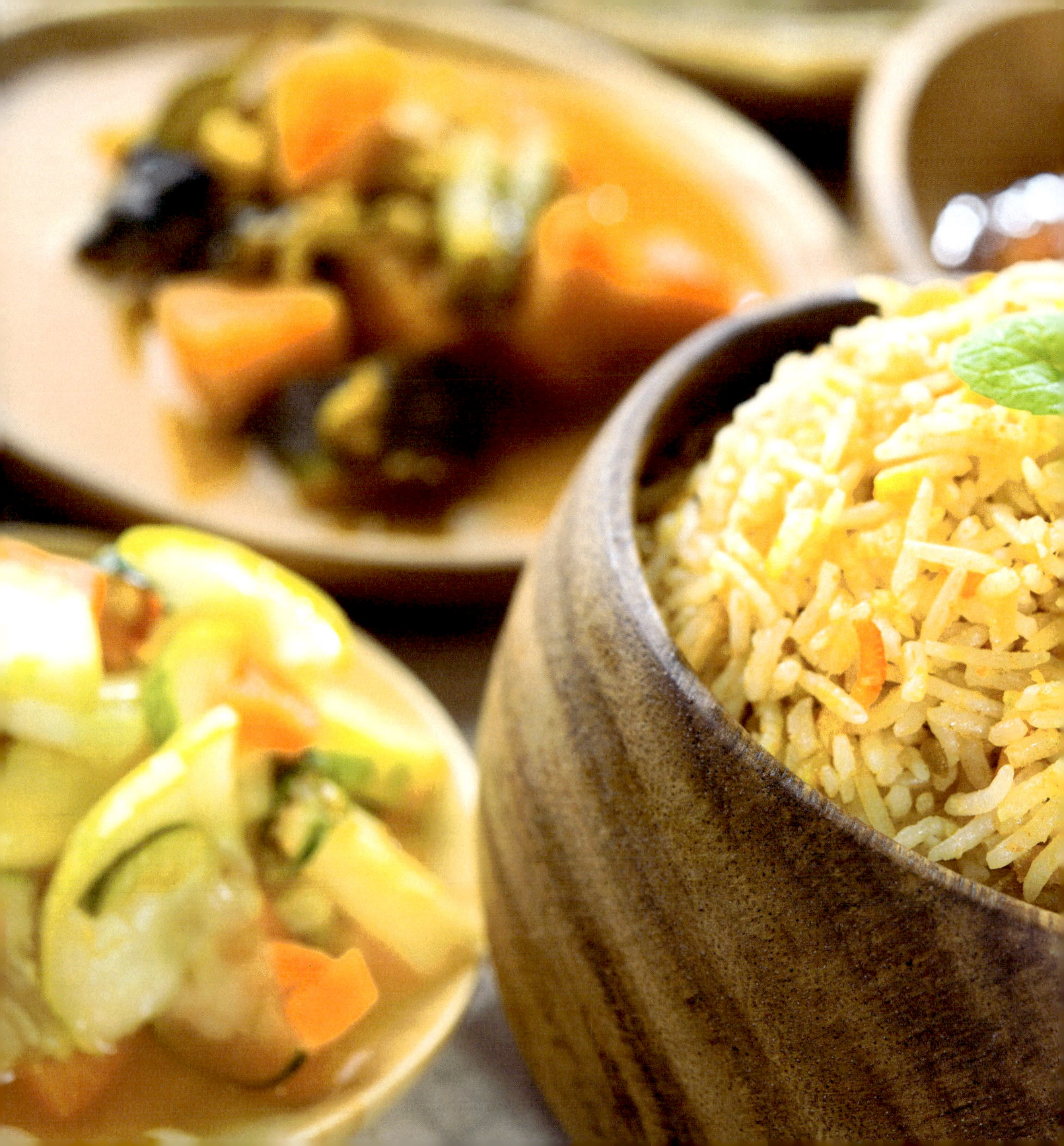

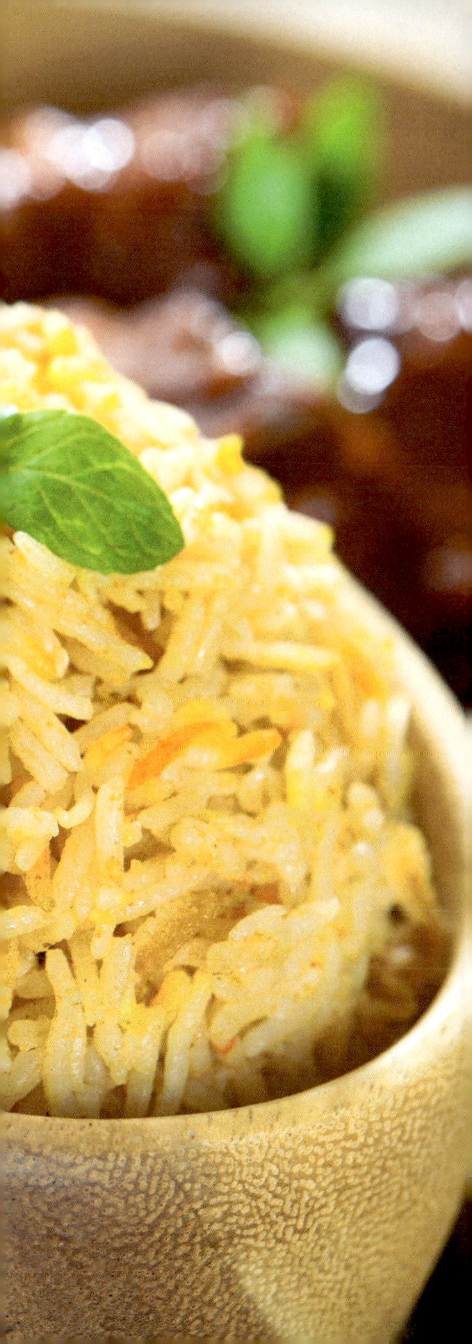

Rice

The recipes below are fool-proof methods for making perfect, fluffy rice every time. When a recipe calls for rice I use the plain recipe and adjust accordingly.

I always use the following quantities -
400g rice to 1 litre (2 pints) water
200g rice to ½ litre (1 pint) water

Basmati Rice

Serves 4

Ingredients

400g Basmati Rice
1 litre boiled water
1 tsp salt

Directions

1. Add the washed rice to the saucepan.

2. Add the boiling, salted water to the pan and boil until almost dry.

3. Turn the heat down to the lowest setting, cover and cook for 6 mins.

4. Serve immediately.

TIP - If you left it too dry before covering cook for 5 mins, if a little moisture is just visible, 6 minutes.

Yellow Rice

Serves 4

Ingredients

400g Basmati Rice
1 litre boiled water
1 tsp salt
1 pinch of yellow food colouring

Directions

1. Add the washed rice to the saucepan.

2. Add the boiling, salted, coloured water to the pan and boil until almost dry.

3. Turn the heat down to the lowest setting, cover and cook for 5-6 mins.

4. Serve immediately.

Turkish Pilaf

Serves 4

Ingredients

400g basmati rice
1 onion finely chopped
3 tbsp currants
3 tbsp cashews or pine nuts
2 tbsp unsalted butter
1 litre boiled water
½ tsp ground cinnamon
1 tsp salt
1 pinch of yellow food colouring

Directions

1. Heat the butter in a large saucepan on a medium heat.

2. Add the chopped onions, nuts and currants and sauté for 5-7 minutes then add the rice.

3. To the boiled water add the salt and ground cinnamon and yellow food colouring. Mix well.

4. Add the boiling, salted water to the pan and boil until almost dry.

5. Turn the heat down to the lowest setting, cover and cook for 6 mins.

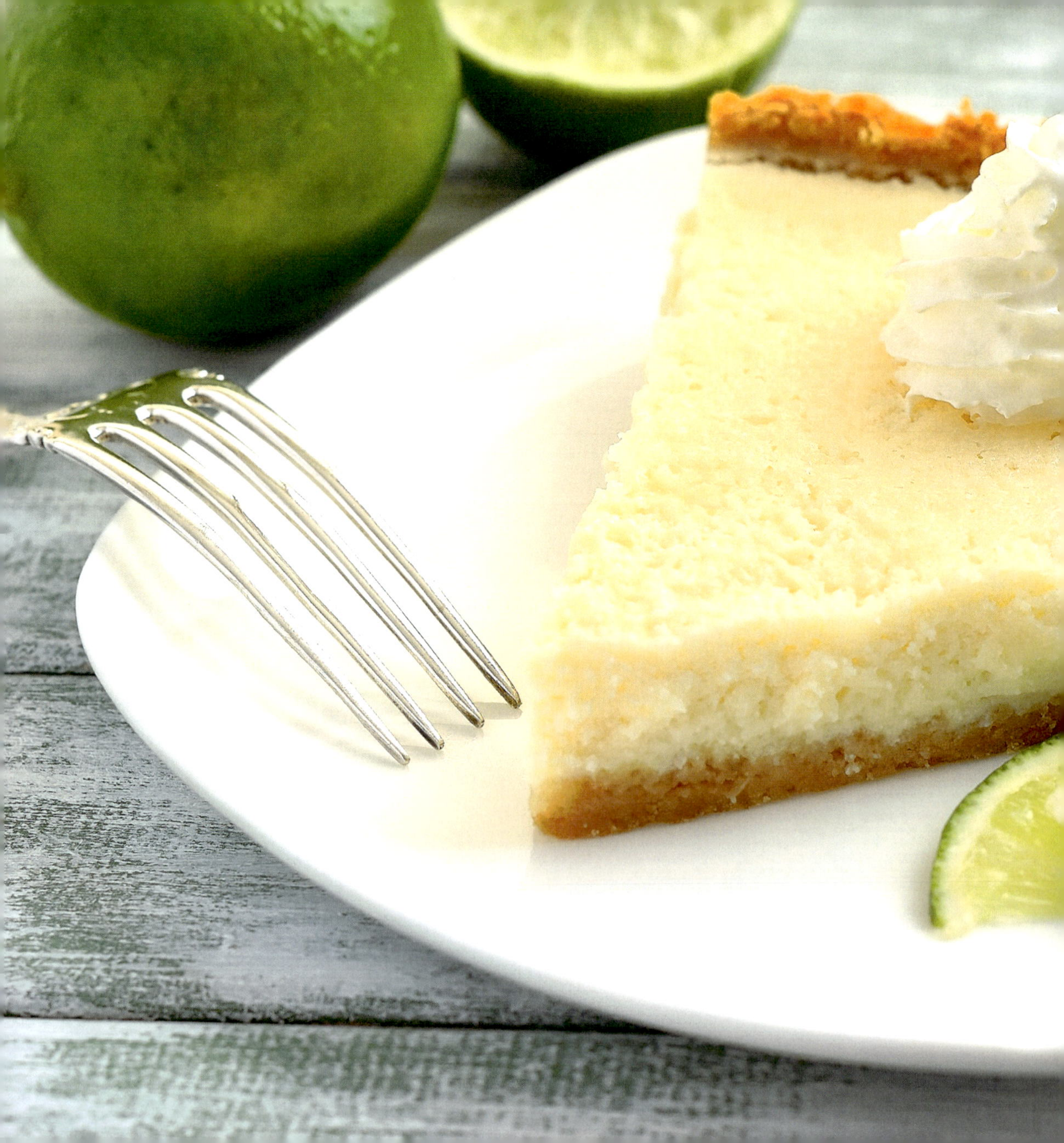

Cakes, Desserts and Perfect Pastry

The Perfect Sponge Cake

Cooking is not a mystery art. It is a matter of being let into a secret. Once you know how it is easy. The art to making a moist sponge every time is in the weighing.
First take the number of eggs you want and weigh them in their shells. If your total eggs (in their shells) weigh 300g you make sure the rest of your basic ingredients are 300g.

So if your eggs weigh 300g you will need –
300g eggs
300g caster sugar
300g self raising flour (sifted)
300g margarine

Serves 4-6

Ingredients

So if your eggs weigh 300g, you will need –
300g eggs
300g caster sugar
300g self raising flour (sifted)
300g margarine

Directions

1. Pre heat the oven to 180 C/350F/Gas mark 4.

2. Grease and line two 7 inch round cake tins with greaseproof paper.

3. Place all your ingredients in a bowl and using the "all in one method" mix well until smooth.

4. Pour the cake mixture into the prepared tins and bake in the middle of the oven for 20 -30 minutes, approximately, until a skewer comes out clean.

5. Turn onto a wire rack and leave until completely cool. The cake can be eaten as is or it can be sandwiched together using butter icing.

Butter Icing

Serves 4-6

Ingredients

100g icing sugar
50g margarine
¼ tsp vanilla essence

Directions

1. Sieve the icing sugar into a bowl.
2. Add the margarine and vanilla essence and beat well.

Perfect Rich Shortcrust Pastry

Ingredients

225g plain flour
pinch salt
115g butter/margarine
1 egg yolk
2 tbsp ice cold water (this is the key)

Directions

1. Sift the flour and salt into a bowl and rub in the butter/margarine.

2. Mix the egg yolk and the iced water and add to the dough mixture.

3. Mix to a firm dough.

4. Wrap in cling film and chill in the fridge for at least 30 minutes.

Use as required.

Lemon & Lime Cream Tart

Serves 4-6

Ingredients

1 tart shell, baked blind
8 large free-range eggs
340g caster sugar
350ml double cream
200ml lime juice
100ml lemon juice

Directions

With this particular tart, as it has a moist filling, its important to egg wash the uncooked tart shell before adding the filling. This adds a waterproof layer and keeps the pastry crisp and short for longer.

1. Whisk together the sugar and eggs in a bowl. When they are well mixed slowly stir in the cream and juices.

2. Put the cooked tart shell back into the oven and then pour the filling into it. This reduces spillage.

3. Bake for around 40 to 45 minutes at 180C/350F/Gas 4 or until the filling is set, but still semi-wobbly in the middle. Different ovens will cook at different rates so it is a good idea to try this tart a couple of times to gauge exactly when you should take it out of the oven.

4. After cooling for an hour the semi-wobbly filling will have firmed up to the perfect consistency; soft and smooth. If you cut it before it has had time to rest it will pour out or be extremely gooey.

5. You can dust it with a little icing sugar if you wish.

6. Serve with cream or ice-cream if desired.

Chocolate Chip Oat Cookies

Makes 20

Ingredients

100g butter/margarine (plus extra for greasing)
100g soft brown sugar
75g self raising flour
100g rolled oats
50g dark chocolate chips

Directions

1. Preheat oven to 180C/350F/Gas Mark 4.

2. Cream the butter and sugar until light and fluffy. Then beat in the flour and stir in the oats, followed by the chocolate chips.

3. Taking heaped teaspoons of the mixture roll into balls between the palms of your hands.

4. Place the balls well apart on a greased baking tray and flatten with the back of a fork.

5. Bake for 10-12 minutes.

6. Remove from the oven and allow to cool slightly before placing on a wire rack to finish cooling.

PLEASE NOTE – The oat cookies should come out of the oven when they are slightly gooey. Leaving them in for any longer than the agreed time will result in rock hard biscuits and not soft and chewy cookies.

Mango, Lime and Coconut Rice Pudding

Serves 4-6

Ingredients

250g pudding rice
400ml tin of coconut milk
80g caster sugar
1 vanilla pod slit in half lengthways
2-3 tbsp desiccated coconut
1 ripe mange or tin of chopped pineapple
150ml double cream

To serve:
Handful of chopped pistachio nuts,
Zest of 1 lime

Directions

1. Put the rice, coconut milk, sugar and vanilla pod into a saucepan. Bring to a simmer, stirring frequently. Then cover the pan and cook for about 20 minutes until the rice is tender. Add more coconut milk if required.

2. Lightly toast the dessicated coconut in a dry frying pan over a medium heat until golden brown, shaking pan frequently to avoid burning. Tip onto a plate and leave to cool.

3. Peel the mango and cut the flesh into small chunks.

4. When the rice is ready, remove the pan from the heat.

5. Stir in the toasted coconut, double cream and half the mango pieces until evenly combined.

6. Cover and stand for 2-3 minutes.

7. Divide between serving bowls and scatter the remaining mango pieces and chopped pistachio nuts on top. Lightly grate over some lime zest and serve.

Index

A
A to Z of Herbs and Spices — 8-13

B
Basmati Rice — 48
Bengali Prawn Curry — 41
Butter Icing — 53

C
Cakes, Desserts and Perfect Pastry — 50
Chicken Madras — 34
Chilli Pumpkin Soup — 22
Chocolate Chip Oat Cookies — 56
Contents — 05
Cumin Kofte Stew — 32

F
Fish and Shellfish — 38
Fish Tenga — 42
Foreword — 07

G
Grilled Spiced Moroccan Chicken — 33

H
Hummus — 21

K
Kofte Kebabs — 31

L
Leek and Chickpea Soup — 19
Lemon and Lime Cream Tart — 55

M
Mango, Lime and Coconut Rice Pudding — 57
Marinated Griddled Tuna Steaks — 40

M
Masala Aloo	29
Meat and Poultry	24
Mercimek Corbasi (Red Lentil Soup)	20
Moroccan Leg Of Lamb	35

P
Perfect Pastry	54
Popcorn Chicken Strips	30
Prawn and Sweetcorn Chowder	18

R
Rice	46

S
Soups and Starters	16
Sponge Cake	52
Spicy Chicken Breast in Semolina	26
Spicy Kidneys	27
Spicy Lamb Chops	28

T
Thai Green Chicken (or Prawn) Curry	36
Turkish Pilaf	49

U
Useful Information	14

Y
Yasmin's Ginger Beer Battered Fish	44
Yasmin's Thai Fish Cakes	43
Yellow Rice	49

Lightning Source UK Ltd.
Milton Keynes UK
UKRC01n1512180117
292309UK00008B/83